Goodbye to Grandpa Geezer Goose

Copyright © 2021
All rights reserved.
Goodbye to Grandpa Geezer Goose
Author: Mary Ellen Lucas
Illustrator: Mikaela San Pietro
Paperback ISBN: 978-1-945026-89-8
Library of Congress Control Number: 2021942050
Published by Owlet Books, an imprint of Sacred Stories Publishing
Fort Lauderdale, FL, USA
Printed in the United States of America

Goodbye to Grandpa Geezer Goose

Mary Ellen Lucas

Illustrations By
Mikaela San Pietro

Love to Linda and Team Sean,
my gratitude always

Chapter One

Grandpa Geezer Goose was a creature of habit. He kept to the same routine day in and day out. He paddled Little Puddle Pond's perimeter visiting neighbors. He roved through the grove waving to the goslings at Goose-a-Garden Grove.

He sauntered slowly over to Peaceful Point Park to do some people watching. Grandpa Geezer Goose found human beings endlessly entertaining!

As the oldest member of the flock, Grandpa Geezer Goose was known as the goose-storian of Little Puddle Pond. Grampy, as he was affectionately called, was born and raised on the pond. He remembered every goose that had ever lived there. He could recall all the geese that had ever come to visit Little Puddle Pond and recount everything that had ever happened.

As a skilled storyteller, Grampy knew how to spruce up a saga with outlandish outrageous flourishes. Sometimes his stories got a little muddled, a little jumbled, a little scrambled around the facts; yet no one ever minded for every creature on Little Puddle Pond loved Grampy.

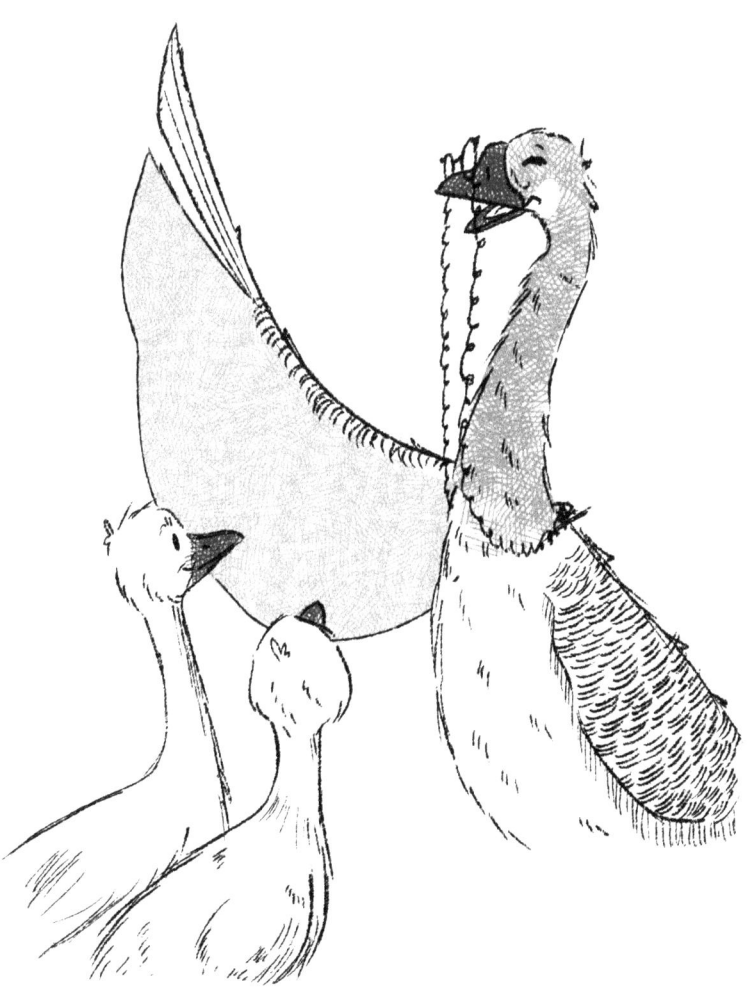

Chapter Two

By the end of the autumn season, Little Puddle Pond would be completely blanketed by a colorful quilt of leaves. Grampy was eager for that to happen for it was then that the Lucky Labyrinth Dash took place. Until then, watching the growing patchwork of colors appear on the pond pleased Grampy.

Each day during his daily jaunt paddling around the pond, he would take note of how many leaves were left on the trees. Grampy would stop for a few moments, captivated by the colorful array of yellow, orange, and red leaves remaining on the trees. Some leaves lost their grip and flew away fast from the swaying tree branches. Down they would fall freely and gracefully onto the pond. A few stubborn leaves held onto the tree branches in spite of the wind's best efforts.

"Don't be afraid," Grampy whispered to the leaves on the trees, "It's okay to let go."

Grampy's attention was next drawn to the goslings playing in the field beside Goose-a-Garden Grove. Harry Honker, a favorite teacher at the school, had used his big honker of a beak to pile up one huge, highly-heaped hill of leaves. Running and jumping, the goslings took turns tumbling and diving into the leaves. Then the little squirts stuffed their beaks to the brim with leaves and ran back to their friends to spew a shower of leaves over their heads. Amused by the antics of the goslings, Grampy, who was known to never pass up a chance to have fun, flew to the field at Goose-a-Garden Grove.

Chapter Three

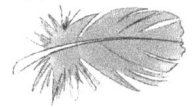

Harry Honker and the goslings honked happily as they welcomed Grampy to their class outing. Grampy thought he'd show these whippersnappers the fanciest dive they would ever see. Even though it was years ago when Professor Foray had taught Grampy how to do a soaring-swirling-somersault dive, he knew he remembered the how-to. Off Grampy ran towards the mound of leaves.

"Watch me!" he yelled excitedly over his shoulder to the goslings.

Grampy's gallop gathered up speed. Just when Grampy was almost at the edge of the pile of leaves, surprisingly, he sprightly sprang straight up and soared solidly upwards as he launched his body over the mound of leaves. Whirling his wings around his knees, he tucked his head down

to go faster. Grampy swirled downwards doing a somersault and then another somersault before he landed feet-first smack dab into the middle of the leaf pile! The goslings cheered. They had never seen a goose do a somersault before. They didn't even know a goose could do a somersault!

Grampy emerged from the pile, took a bow, and wing-brushed the leaves off as he walked back to his adoring audience. Grampy gave a knowing wink to Harry Honker and said,

"It's time for the goslings to learn what Professor Foray taught me many years ago. To have the best fun in autumn, they must learn the soaring-swirling-somersault maneuver."

Harry Honker agreed and let Grampy teach the goslings the rest of the afternoon. The goslings learned how to dash forward, spring upward, propel properly and steadily soar until they were over the pile. Next, they swirled swiftly into a somersault as they smashed safely back down into the cushion of leaves. The goslings thanked Grampy for teaching them how to have the best fun ever!

"When the pond holds the annual Lucky Labyrinth Dash," Grampy enthusiastically said, "I'll see you there and cheer you on from the sidelines."

One of the goslings piped up, "I'm going to be the winner this year!"

Grampy chuckled and encouraged all the goslings, "The Dash sure is a dandy magic maze. You might get confused but give it your best. You'll be sure to have fun!"

Chapter Four

One fine autumn day, Professor Foray swam by to visit his old friend Grampy. Professor Foray had heard all about Grampy's grand adventure with the goslings at Goose-a-Garden Grove's field. Professor Foray was tickled Grampy still knew how to do the soaring-swirling-somersault maneuver. He got a kick out of imagining Grampy at his age being able to accomplish such a fine feat.

"You sure are spry for an old codger," Professor Foray chuckled.

"No matter my age," winked Grampy, "I'll always be young at heart."

"Yes, you will," Professor Foray agreed.

"Will you be coming to the Lucky Labyrinth Dash?" asked Grampy.

"Yes, I will," Professor Foray replied as he waved goodbye, "see you then!"

Onward Professor Foray swam to go visit his former student Willie. He was curious to see if Willie would remember the famous two-web-foot goose kick he had taught him many years ago.

As autumn days began to edge closer to winter, Grampy noticed how the colder temperatures tested his mettle. One day Grampy was startled to realize he no longer was able to keep his daily routine. He huffed and puffed as he swam around Little Puddle Pond. A hovering huff, a persistent puff, led Grampy to admit he was not feeling up to snuff. These days once around the pond was all he could muster.

Soon Grampy began to notice how extremely tired he felt. It was difficult to lift his wing to wave a friendly "Hi" to the other geese. He knew that without being

able to do a wing lift his flying days would be over.

The daily routines Grampy had lived by were now no longer possible. He felt very, very sad. Grampy made a plan. Whenever his tiredness grew too much and it became too hard to move, he would go to a quiet secluded spot in the bushes. Grampy would follow the examples of the leaves.

All that was necessary was to let go and gracefully float away. Until that day came, Grampy promised to live each day with gratitude for the life he had.

Chapter Five

The Talking Spot in the middle of Little Puddle Pond was the gathering place to get the latest gossip. Gabby Goose, a busy goosey-body into everyone else's business, spread the news about Grampy's terrible tuckered-out tiredness.

The next day Glossie, the leader of the flock, echoed a commanding honk for all to meet at the Talking Spot. Once gathered, Glossie queried the geese, "How can we help Grampy?"

Lucy, once the pond's loosey-goosey goose-sitter, who had matured into a generous, thoughtful goose, offered to check-in daily on Grampy. Lucy knew it

had become too hard for Grampy to forage for food for himself, so she organized friends to deliver a daily dollop of delicious food. Friends came by with meals of berries, grasses, seeds, and grains. Grampy sure appreciated the flock's care.

Whenever Grampy saw Lucy, his eyes lit up. Lucy sure brightened up his day! One day Lucy was surprised to see a flower perched on Grampy's head just like the flower Lucy always wore.

"What a silly goose you are," Lucy laughingly said to Grampy as he beamed back to a her a big beaked smile.

Soon the time came when the flock noticed how feeble and fragile Grampy had become. Wanting to ease their sadness, Grampy reassured them, "Everything changes. Nothing stays the same, I have lived a good long life. I'll know when it's time to leave. All I have to do is let go just like the leaves in autumn do and follow the light from the sun."

Chapter Six

Grampy relished the pond's view of the sun's golden rays highlighting the magnificent colors on the leaves. The sky was a brilliant blue with not a wisp of cloud to be seen. He swam slowly over to the bushes at the north side of the pond. A few geese spied Grampy as he slowly stepped onto the shore bank. They didn't know what Grampy knew. He had just taken his final swim in his beloved waters of Little Puddle Pond.

Grampy found an open spot in the middle of the bushes and lay gently down on the earth. He thought about what he had learned as a gosling: there is no limit to the horizon. Grampy looked up at the vast expanse of sky stretched out endlessly above and knew his spirit would soon soar up and away. Unlike other journeys flown

with his flock, this journey was meant to be traveled alone. Grampy thought about his friends who had made this journey before him and how he had enjoyed telling stories about them. He knew his friends would enjoy telling a story or two about him when he was gone.

Next to the bushes where Grampy lay, a cattail camouflage hid Bella Blue Heron. She stood still silently watching Grampy as he gazed upward at the sky, staring at a faraway point. Then Grampy turned his head to take one long, last look at Little Puddle Pond, the place he had called home his whole life.

Grampy thought how lucky he had been in his life. He wondered how he could feel so grateful and so sad at the same time. Then he turned his gaze away from Little Puddle Pond and looked up again at the limitless sky.

Chapter Seven

Meanwhile Lucy, who had swum over to check on Grampy, got nervous when she couldn't find him. She searched around the pond but no one else had seen Grampy either. However, everyone did notice the sudden appearance of Bella Blue Heron

flying hurriedly over to the Talking Spot. No one had ever seen Bella Blue Heron's wings flap so quickly as she flew through the air, squawking the loudest shriek anyone had ever heard. Curious, everyone gathered around to hear what she had to say.

"Grampy's gone," Bella Blue Heron cried. The flock was heartbroken.

A day was planned to honor the passing of Grandpa Geezer Goose. Bruce the Goose flew over from Middle Puddle Pond and huddled with his long-time friends Nellie and Willie. Led by Harry Honker and Professor Foray, the goslings walked over from Goose-a-Garden Grove. Glossie planned to lead the flock in a fly-over tribute to Grampy. The airborne geese would give a one-wing salute as they flew over Little Puddle Pond. The goslings would wave back just like Grampy used to wave to them.

There weren't enough honking hankies to hold back the flood of tears bursting forth from all those who had loved Grampy. Tears flowed freely, so much so, that the pond spilled over the banks of Little Puddle Pond.

Seemingly from out of nowhere, a single goose feather floated down and landed smack dab in the middle of their midst. All eyes turned upward to see which goose had just flown by. Who had lost a feather?

Where did the feather come from? The flummoxed flock became confused. There was no goose to be seen!

Chapter Eight

Before Grampy died, Mother Goose had been chosen to be the pond's next goose-storian. Mother Goose heard all the stories Grampy had stored in his heart throughout his years on Little Puddle Pond. Grampy told her the legendary tale about the day Nellie and Willie stopped their silly goose squabbling. Mother Goose could scarcely believe all the foolish choices the goslings Glossie and Flossie made before they finally learned to listen to their GPS or inner Goose Pause Setting. Mother Goose soon learned a variety of stories about each creature on Little Puddle Pond and those who had visited.

The flock invited Mother Goose to speak at Grampy's celebration of life ceremony. Mother Goose began by reminding the flock that Grampy knew his story didn't end with his death.

"He's still watching over us," Mother Goose stated. "He promised he'd drop a feather down from above so you'd be sure to find it. If you ever come across a single feather, it's a sign from Grampy meant to lighten your heart."

The geese gawked at Mother Goose. Baffled earlier about the falling feather, now they understood the meaning of the one feather floating down from the sky. It was a sign from Grampy!

"Remembering Grampy keeps him alive," Mother Goose said.

She then talked fondly about his daily jaunts and the naps he would take under the oak tree. It was Grampy's favorite dozing place to snooze despite Seanie, the bushy-tailed squirrel's constant chitter-chattering above his head.

"The last conversation I had with Grampy," Mother Goose shared, "he told me he knew he was dying, yet he was at peace. He's a part of the circle of life and will continue on in a new place, just as those here will continue on until their journey has been completed. Today we celebrate the many years we had with Grampy and the love we shared."

Mother Goose and the flock on Little Puddle Pond continued to tell stories about Grampy. Sometimes the stories made them very sad, for they all missed seeing Grampy. Sometimes thinking about Grampy made them cry. Mother Goose reminded the flock that it was okay to feel sad.

"Of course, you will miss someone who was loved dearly. No matter what you are feeling, it's okay."

Once in a while, a goose would come across a single feather, smile knowingly, and share with the others that Grampy had sent his regards. The geese would chuckle and their hearts felt lighter thinking of Grampy and how they still loved him.

Chapter Nine

Now that the pond was fully covered with a thick layer of leaves, the long-awaited Lucky Labyrinth Dash was held. Bella Blue Heron's broad beak pushed leaves aside to form multiple pathways. The goslings' goal was to race through the leaf labyrinth to find the one pathway that opened into a leaf-free clear area of the pond. There Willie lay in wait for the first gosling to arrive, who then would be declared the winner of the Lucky Labyrinth Dash.

Everyone in the flock thought about how Grampy had delighted in Dash day and would laugh heartily as he watched the goslings' fun! They sure missed seeing

him at the Dash.

The goslings, amazed by the maze, swam the leaf labyrinth over and over again. They didn't really care who won, for they remembered that Grampy used to say, "It doesn't matter who comes in first. You'll always be a winner as long as you do your best."

Life continued on for Little Puddle Pond, and even though Grampy was gone from their sight, he was never far from their thoughts. Memories of Grampy filled their hearts with happiness, though sometimes sad tears still splashed out from their eyes. If you miss someone who is no longer alive, Mother Goose would say this means you loved them well. And Grampy would say, "Loving someone mightily is the greatest story of all."

About the Author

Photo credit: Ryan Bassett

Mary Ellen Lucas is an Interfaith / Interspiritual Minister. She resides in Northeast Ohio with a backyard view of a pond where she observes the Canadian geese she writes about. Their silly antics inspired her children's book series Life on Little Puddle Pond. Her stories are full of fun as well as gently addressing many relevant themes. This is her third book in the series which subtly portrays her belief in life after death and how there is an ongoing connection with loved ones even after they die. She believes our loved ones send us signs in order for us to know that love lives on and never truly dies.

CPSIA information can be obtained
at www.ICGtesting.com
Printed in the USA
BVHW051339031021
617774BV00012BA/483